Out of the Mouth

# Out of the Mouth of Babes

A SELECTION OF CHILDREN'S THOUGHTS ON GOD,
THE CHURCH AND LIFE COLLECTED BY

## DAVID PYTCHES

CARTOONS BY TAFFY DAVIES

eagle

Guildford, Surrey

Text: Copyright © 1999 David Pytches
Cartoons: Copyright © 1999 Taffy Davies

The right of David Pytches to be identified as compiler of this work has been asserted by him in accordance with the Copyright, Design and Patents Act 1988.

British Library Cataloguing in Publication Data. A catalogue record for this book is available from the British Library.

Published by Eagle, an imprint of Inter Publishing Service (IPS) Ltd, PO Box 530, Guildford, Surrey GU2 5FH.

Typeset by Eagle Publishing
Printed by Gutenberg Press, Malta
ISBN No:    0 86347 347 4

## CHILDREN'S LETTERS TO GOD . . .

Dear God:
Did you mean the giraffe to look like that or was it an accident?
  Norma

Dear God:
Instead of letting people die and having to make new ones, why don't you just keep the ones you have now?
  Jane

Dear God:
I went to this wedding and they kissed right in church. Is that OK?
  Tom

Dear God:
Thank you for my baby brother,
but what I prayed for was a puppy.
Joan


Dear God:
Please send me a pony.
I never asked for anything before.
You can look it up.
Harry

Dear God:
It rained for the whole of our holiday and is my father mad! He said some things about you that people are not supposed to say, but I hope you will not hurt him anyway.

> Your friend
> (but I am not going to tell you who I am)

Dear God:
I bet it's very hard for you to love all the people in the world. There are only four people in our family and I can never do it.

> Jan

Dear God:
My brothers told me about being born, but it doesn't sound right. They are just kidding aren't they?

> Marilyn

Dear God:
If you watch me in church on Sunday, I'll show you my new shoes.
                                                    Mike


Dear God:
We read that Thomas Edison made light. But in Sunday School we learned that you did it. So I bet he stole your idea.
                                                    June


Dear God:
I didn't think that orange went with purple until I saw the sunset you made last night. That was cool.
                                                    Hilary


Dear God:
Maybe Cain and Abel would not kill each other so much if they had their own rooms. It works with my brother.
                                                    Peter

One Sunday a young child was playing up so much during church that his father eventually had to pick him up and carry him out. As the father marched sternly down the aisle the boy called out loudly to the congregation: 'Pray for me! Pray for me!'

The event was a school nativity play and the Angel Gabriel announced his presence to the virgin Mary with the words: 'Hail! Thou that art highly-flavoured . . .'

*Notice in hotel:* Unattended children shall
be sold as slaves.


'I didn't ask God to help me not to misbehave,'
said Alan to his exasperated parents.
'I asked him to help you to put up with me!'

Boy to school chaplain: Christianity has been in the world 2,000 years and look at the state of it.
Chaplain: Water has been in the world longer than that and just look at the state of your neck!


A wise school teacher sends this note to all parents on the first day of school: 'If you promise not to believe everything your child says happens at school, I'll promise not to believe everything he says happens at home.'


'What little boy can tell us the meaning of the expression "The quick and the dead?" ' asked the Sunday school teacher.

'Please, ma'am,' Willie said, 'the quick are the ones that get out of the way of cars, and the dead are the ones that don't.'

A father overheard his child addressing God as 'Dear Harold' and interrupted him to find out why. 'Well, that's what we call him in church,' said the little boy. 'You know the prayer "Our Father who art in Heaven, Harold be thy name!" '

A rabbi to a precocious six-year-old said: 'So your mother says your prayers for you each night? Very good. What does she say?' The little boy replied: 'Thank God he's in bed!'

The lads had decided to go fishing on Sunday morning. All turned up on time except Danny. He finally arrived ten minutes late. 'It was a toss-up as to whether I went to church or joined you guys fishing.' 'Well, that shouldn't have taken you so long!' 'But I had to toss up 27 times!'

After the Christmas morning service, the baby Jesus was missing from the crib. The vicar was searching for him when a little girl arrived with a doll's pram and started lifting the baby Jesus out and putting him back into the crib saying: 'I told you that if I got a pram for Christmas you would be the first to get a ride in it!'

*(Mrs B. King, Westbridgeford, Notts)*

One Baptist to another: Do you believe in infant baptism?
Second Baptist: Believe in it? I've actually seen it done!

'Mum,' said the little boy; 'where did I come from?'
'The stork brought you, dear,' she replied.
'And where did you come from, Mummy?'
'The stork brought me too.'
'And what about grandma?'
'The stork brought her too.'
'Wow, Mum!' said the little lad. 'Doesn't it ever worry you to think that there have been no natural births in our family for three generations?'


A small boy was asking his mother where he came from and when he heard his mother's explanation he said: 'Mummy, when God planted the seed in your tummy, was there a photo of me on the packet?'

15

Teacher (answering the phone): I see – little Johnnie
can't come to school today because he's got a fever.
To whom am I speaking, please?
Voice: This is my father.


'Mum where do babies come from?'
'From the stork of course.'
'But who gets the stork pregnant?'

'Dear Santa Claus: I wanna put in a new order quick as I just found all those things which I asked you for under the spare-room bed.'

A little boy was praying: 'Dear God, please take care of my daddy and my mummy and my sister and brother and my doggy and me. Oh, please take care of yourself, God. If anything happens to you, we're gonna be in a big mess.'

| Teacher: | Have you ever heard of Julius Caesar? |
| Pupil: | Yes, sir. |
| Teacher: | What do you think he would be doing now, if he were alive? |
| Pupil: | Drawing an old-age pension. |

The minister was leading in prayer at church when a little boy suddenly whistled very loudly. All heads turned in his direction. The embarrassed mother was horrified and pinched him to silence. After church she remonstrated: 'Whatever made you do such a thing?' Matter-of-factly the little boy replied: 'I asked God to teach me to whistle and he did just then!'

A little boy excited about his part in the Christmas play came home and said:
'I got a part in the Christmas play!'
'What part?' asked his mother.
'I'm one of the three wise guys!' was the reply.

A parent overheard his child praying by his bedside: 'Now I lay me down to rest; I hope to pass tomorrow's test. If I should die before I wake, that's one less test I have to take.'

The teacher explained to her class that Joseph and Mary had to sleep in the stable, because there was no room at the inn. A little boy piped up: 'I blame Joseph, Miss. He should have booked in advance like my Dad does.'

An agent for double-glazing made a random call to a house and a little child picked up the phone:

'Is your mother in?'

'Yes!' the child whispered.

'Can you get her for me please?'

'No!' the child whispered again. 'Why not?'

'She's busy,' whispered the child.

'Oh, then is your father in?'

'Yes!' the child whispered.

'Can you get him for me?'

'No!'

'Why not?'

'Because he's busy,' she continued in a whisper.

'Well, do you have any other grown-up relative in the house?'

'Yes. My auntie.'

'Can you fetch her please?'

'No.'

'Why not?'

'She's busy,' the child continued in a whisper.

'Well, is there any other grown up in the house?'

'Yes!' – still in a whisper.

'Who is that?'

'It's a policeman.'

'Oh! Can you call the policeman?'

'No!'

'Why not?'

'He's busy,' she replied, still speaking in a whisper.

There was a pause and then the salesman tried one last tack: 'All these people are busy. Can you tell me what they are so busy doing?'

'Yes,' she whispered, 'they are busy looking for me!'


Be nice to your kids. They'll choose your
nursing home.

The parents felt that at last they could leave Johnny at home with Granny while they went abroad for their first holiday alone for years. By the time three days were up Mother was anxious and phoned home to find out how things were.

'How are you, Johnny darling?'

'Fine,' said Johnny 'everything's fine, except that the cat's dead.'

Mother was grief-stricken with the shock of this sudden tragedy and left the phone weeping copious tears over the unexpected loss of her very precious pet.

The father was shocked to find her so distraught and went back to the phone to finish the conversation, using the opportunity just to coax his son into a better way of breaking bad news.

'Look son, I know you have little experience in this area but bad news needs to be broken gradually – your mother needed some kind of warning to soften the blow. What you might have said was something along the lines of "Well the cat's on the garage roof and I can't get her down.' The next day you could add that the cat's not eating. Finally, at the next call, you can break the bad news. Do see what I'm getting at, son?'

'Yes, Dad – I see. I'm so sorry.'

Three days later, Mother phoned again to hear the latest news from home. 'Hello Johnny! How are you?'

'Fine,' said Johnny, 'yes, everything is fine, except that Granny's on the garage roof and I can't get her down!'

'Mum, you know that vase you were worried I might break?'

'Yes, what about it?'

'Well, your worries are over.'

A little boy was overheard praying: 'Lord, if you can't make me a better boy, don't worry about it. I'm having a real good time like I am!'

Nervous head boy reading a Lesson in School Assembly:
'Here beginneth the first Actor of the Chaps.'

## SCHOOL-BOY HOWLERS

*(collected by Sutton Valence, a school chaplain)*

The fish swam down the coast in shawls.

In answer to the teacher's question about which part of the 'Armour of God' was sharp and cutting, one child replied, 'The axe of the apostles'.

*Jesus said:* 'If you want to divorce your wife leave a note for her on the table!'

Some of the seed was curried off by Satan.

The Kingdom of God is no ordinary place like the bathroom at home.

Jesus cured the man with the withered arm by spitting at him and putting his fingers in his ears.

After he had denied Jesus, Peter was so upset that
he went and hung himself upside down.


Jesus healed a man with a weathered hand.


An altar is a stall for candles.


*Jesus said:* 'It is better that he should be thrown into
the sea with a milestone around his neck.'

The last verses of Mark's Gospel were written later by a unanimous person.

Jesus first proclaimed the gospel to the Jews: he told them to make love to each other.

In a wedding the bride walks down the aisle to meet her father.

The nave is the space where no one sits.

The main purpose of the prophets was to set up the lights for when Jesus came on the stage.

An example of Holy Orders are the Ten Commandments.

## CHILDREN (THE THINGS THEY SAY)

It was her first wedding and the little girl was so excited and curious about everything she could not stop asking her mother questions. 'Why is the bride all dressed in white?' she whispered.

Her mother explained that white was the colour of happiness. 'And this is the happiest day of her life.'

'Oh,' the child retorted, 'then why is the groom all dressed in black?'

He was dressed in the garbage of a monk –
(school-girl).

Pins have saved many lives by people
not swallowing them – (school-boy).

Salome danced in front of Harrods.

Lot's wife was a pillar of salt by day and a ball
of fire by night.

If Mrs Jones does not have her baby soon I expect she'll have to be seduced – (two small girls talking).

I told my young boy to go to the end of the line but he came back and said: 'Dad there's someone already there.'

Teacher: 'How much is six and four?'
Boy: 'That's about eleven ain't it?'
Teacher: 'Six and four are ten.'
Boy: 'But six and four can't be ten.
Five and five are ten.'

'Dad,' said a little boy, 'you know Mum has no idea about how to bring up children.'
'Whatever makes you say that?' replied his father.
'Well she sends me to bed when I'm not sleepy and tells me to get up when I am still tired!'

The purpose of John's baptism was to make people into proper Christians before the Messiah came.

## QUESTIONNAIRE PUT TO CHILDREN IN THE USA

Q:      'How does a person decide who to marry?'
A. (1)  'You flip a nickel, and heads means you stay with him and tails means you try the next one.'

(Sally aged 9)

A. (2)  'You've got to find somebody who likes the same stuff. Like if you like sports, she should like it that you like sports, and she should keep the chips and dip coming.'

(Allan aged 10)

A. (3)  'No person really decides before they grow up who they're going to marry. God decides it all way before, and you got to find out later who you're stuck with.'

(Kirsten aged 10)

Q. 'What's the best age to get married?'
A. 'Twenty-three is the best age because you know the person FOREVER by then.'
(Kirsten aged 10)


Q. 'How can a stranger tell if two people are married?'
A. 'You might have to guess based on whether they seem to be yelling at the same kids!'
(Derrick aged 9)

Q.    'What do you think your mom and dad have in common?'
A.    'Both don't want no more kids!'

(Lori aged 8)


Q.    'When is it OK to kiss?'
A.    'The law says you have to be eighteen, so I wouldn't want to mess with that.'

(Curt, aged 7)


Q.    'What do people do on dates?'
A. (1) 'Dates are for having fun, and people should use them to get to know each other. Even boys have something to say if you listen long enough.'

(Lynette aged 8)

A. (2) 'On the first date they just tell each other lies, and that usually gets them interested enough to go for a second date.'

Q. 'What would you do on a first date that was turning sour?'

A. 'I'd run home and play dead. The next day I would call all the newspapers and make sure they wrote about me in all the dead columns.'

(Craig aged 9)

Q. 'What promises do a man and woman make when they get married?'

A. 'A man and a woman promise to go through sickness and illness and disease together.'

(Marlon aged 10)

Q.     'What advice do you have for a young couple about to be married?'

A.     'The first thing I'd say to them is: Listen up, young 'uns. I got something to say to you. Why in the heck do you wanna get married anyway?'

(Craig aged 9)


Q.     'Is it better to be single or married?'

A. (1) 'It's better for girls to be single but not for boys. Boys need somebody to clean up after them!'

(Anita)

A. (2) 'Single is better . . . for the simple reason that I wouldn't want to change no diapers . . . Of course if I did get married, I'd figure something out. I'd just phone my mother and have her come over for some coffee and diaper-changing.'

(Kirsten aged 10)

Q.    'What do think about getting married the second time?'
A.    'Most men are brainless, so you might have to try more than one to find a live one.'

(Angie aged 10)


Q.    'How do you make a marriage last?'
A. (1) 'Tell your wife that she looks pretty even if she looks like a truck!'

(Ricky aged 7)

A. (2) 'If you want to last with your man, you should wear a lot of sexy clothes, especially underwear that is red and maybe has a few diamonds on it!'

(Lori aged 8)

40

A gladiator is something that keeps the room warm.

An easel is a small but vicious rodent.

In some countries people are put to death by elocution.

A saint is a dead clergyman.

When letters are in sloping type they are in hysterics.

An antidote is a funny story you have heard before.

The Tropic of Cancer is a rare and dangerous disease.

Q. 'How would the world be different if people didn't get married?'

A. (1) 'There sure would be a lot of kids to explain, wouldn't there?'

(Kevin aged 8)

A. (2) 'You can be sure of one thing – the boys would come chasing after us just as they do now!'

(Roberta aged 7)

Philosophy is being able to explain why you are happy when you are poor.


Ali Baba means being somewhere else when the crime was committed


Little boy: 'I wonder how old Sally is?'
Small girl: 'I bet she won't see four again.'

Boy: 'Please, teacher, my two-year-old brother
tore up my composition!'
Teacher: 'What! Can he read already?'

Teacher to new pupil: 'Do you know your
alphabet?'
William: 'Yes, Miss.'
Teacher: 'What comes after "A"?'
William: 'All the rest of them!'

A boy was being encouraged by his teacher to try his hand at some poetry so he sat down and composed the following rhyme:

A boy was walking down the track
The train was coming fast.
The boy stepped off the railway track
to let the train go past.

'Good,' said the teacher, 'but it lacks drama. Try again!'
Johnny came up with the following:

A boy was walking down the track
The train was coming fast
The train jumped off the railway track
To let the boy go past!

Little girl to mother: 'Mummy do you and Daddy have sexual relations?' Mother, caught off guard for a moment, managed a nonchalant admission without seeming too embarrassed. 'Oh yes!' she said, congratulating herself on sounding so cool. 'Then why haven't I ever met any them?' the little girl complained.

Teacher: 'When I was your age I could answer any question in arithmetic.'
William: 'Yes but you had a different teacher.'


Teacher: 'That essay about the dog is exactly the same as your brother's.'
Pupil: 'Well Sir, it is the same dog.'

## THE HISTORY LESSONS THE CHILDREN LEARNED

Ancient Egypt was inhabited by mummies and they all wrote in hydraulics.

The Bible is full of interesting caricatures. In the first book of the Guinesses, Adam and Eve were cremated from an apple tree. One of their children, Cain, asked, 'Am I my brother's son?'

Moses led the Hebrew slaves to the Red Sea, where they made unleavened bread which is bread made without any ingredients.

Finally Magna Carta provided that no man should be hanged twice for the same offence.

The sun never set on the British Empire because the British Empire is in the East and the sun sets in the West.

Solomon had three hundred wives and seven porcupines.

Moses went up on Mount Cyanide to get the ten commandments. He died before he ever reached Canada.

The Greeks were a highly-sculptured people and without them we would not have history. The Greeks also had myths. A myth is a female moth.

Nero was a cruel tyranny who would torture his subjects by playing the fiddle to them.

The greatest writer of the Renaissance was William Shakespeare. He was born in the year 1564, supposedly on his birthday. He never made much money and is famous only because of his plays. He wrote tragedies, comedies and hysterectomies, all in Islamic pentameter. Romeo and Juliet are an example of a heroic couple. Romeo's last wish was to be laid by Juliet.

Later the Pilgrims crossed the ocean, and this was called the Pilgrim's Progress. The winter of 1620 was a hard one for the settlers. Many people died and many babies were born. Captain John Smith was responsible for all this.

Bach was the most famous composer in the world and so was Handel. Handel was half German, half Italian and half English. He was very large.

Napoleon wanted an heir to inherit his power but since Josephine was a baroness she could not have children.

It was an age of great inventions and discoveries. Gutenberg invented removable tape and the Bible.

Socrates was a famous Greek teacher who went around giving people advice. They killed him. After his death his career suffered a dramatic decline.

The First World War, caused by the assignation of the Arch-Duck by an anahist, ushered in a new error in the anals of human history.

Queen Victoria was the longest Queen. She sat on the thorn for 63 years. She was a moral person who practised virtue. Her death was the final event which ended her reign.

Joan of Arc was burnt at the steak and was connonized by Bernard Shaw.

Louis Pasteur discovered a cure for rabies. Charles Darwin was a naturalist who wrote the Organ of the Species. A Madman Curie discovered radio. And Karl Marx become one of the Marx brothers.

## Adults on Kids

Raising kids is like eating grapefruit. No matter how you do it the little squirts get to you.

Tonight I'd like to say a kind word about kids. Do you realise that if you have kids you don't have to hold up a seashell to hear a roar?

It's a little frustrating to listen to your kid, who has already cost you thousands of pounds, say his prayers – and you get mentioned ahead of the goldfish but after the gerbil.

56

Three-year-olds really know how to live: eat, drink and be messy.

I was so surprised by my birth, I was speechless for the first year and a half!

Mealtime is when young children sit down to continue eating.

It's nice for children to have pets, until the pets start having children.

There is just one way to bring up a child in the way he should go, and that is to travel that way yourself. *(Abraham Lincoln)*

Parents are the very last people who ought to be allowed to have children. *(Ted Bell)*

60

Somewhere on this earth a woman is giving birth to a child every ten seconds. We must find this woman and stop her at once. *(Sam Levenson)*

She got her looks from her father – he's a plastic surgeon. *(Groucho Marx)*

Until I was thirteen I thought my name was 'shut up'. *(Joe Namath)*

Father: Don't you think our son gets all his
brains from me?
Mother: Probably. I still have all of mine.


Mother: My child certainly has a lot of original
ideas, doesn't he?
Teacher: Oh, yes, but it is unfortunate they
are in spelling.


Life is full of complications. Even when you are
born there is a string attached.

The children now love luxury; they show disrespect for elders and love chatter in the place of exercise. Children are tyrants, not the servants of their households. They no longer rise when their elders enter the room. They contradict their parents, chatter before company, gobble up dainties at the table, cross their legs and tyrannise their teachers.

*(Socrates, 469–399 BC)*